Scientists

Carlotta Hacker

Weigl

CALGARY
www.weigl.com

Dedication

This series is dedicated to all Canadians who take pride in their communities and their citizenship; and to those who will continue to help build a strong Canada. The Canadians in this series have helped to build Canada by being outstanding in their fields, from literature to business, sports to the arts. Some have overcome great obstacles to make their dreams come true, and their dedication and achievement serve as an inspiration for young and old alike.

Published by Weigl Educational Publishers Limited
6325 - 10 Street SE
Calgary, Alberta, Canada
T2H 2Z0
Web site: http://www.weigl.com
Copyright © 2000 WEIGL EDUCATIONAL PUBLISHERS LIMITED

Canadian Cataloguing in Publication Data

Hacker, Carlotta, 1931–
  Scientists

(Great Canadians)
Includes bibliographical references and index.
ISBN 1-896990-3-7

1. Scientists—Canada—Biography—Juvenile literature. I. Title.
II. Series: Great Canadians (Calgary, Alta.)
Q141.H224 1999   j509'.2'271   C99-910532-9

Printed and bound in Canada
1 2 3 4 5 6 7 8 9 0   03 02 01 00 99

Editor
Leslie Strudwick
Design
Warren Clark
Cover Design
Chris Bowerman
Copy Editor
Rennay Craats
Layout
Lucinda Cage

Photograph Credits

Every reasonable effort has been made to trace ownership and to obtain permission to reprint copyright material. The publishers would be pleased to have any errors or omissions brought to their attention so that they may be corrected in subsequent printings.

The Banting and Best Museum: pages 6, 7, 8, 9, 10; Courtesy Roberta Bondar: cover, pages 12, 13, 15, 16, 17; CP Picture Archive: pages 14, 27; Federal Bureau of Investigation: page 26; Courtesy Filomena Galdikas: page 19; Richard Longley: page 36; Courtesy McMaster University, Public Relations: page 42; Courtesy National Research Council: page 43; Courtesy The Orangutan Foundation International: pages 18, 20, 21, 22, 23; Courtesy John Polyani: page 44; Courtesy Project Seahorse, McGill University: page 45; Courtesy Michael Smith: pages 24, 28, 29; Courtesy Denis St-Onge: pages 30, 31, 32, 33, 34, 35; Courtesy David Suzuki: pages 36, 37, 39, 40, 41.

CONTENTS

6
Frederick Banting and Charles Best

12
Roberta Bondar

18
Biruté Galdikas

24
Michael Smith

30
Denis St-Onge

36
David Suzuki

Scientists

Long before Europeans came to Canada, Aboriginal Peoples practiced their own science. They knew a lot about the world around them, especially about the plants and animals. They knew how to make medicine from plants, and they shared some of this knowledge with early French explorers.

In the 1600s, French settlers brought European science to Canada. The very first settler at Quebec was an **apothecary**, Louis Hébert. Another early scientist was Michel Sarrazin, a **botanist**. When the British came to Canada, they too brought specialists, including **engineers**.

Since those early years, there have been many Canadian scientists in a wide range of fields. Some have gained world fame for their inventions. Alexander Graham Bell (who invented the telephone) and Charles Edward Saunders (who developed Marquis wheat) are just two of the many.

This book is about more recent scientists. Most of the people described here are still very active in their fields. They represent a selection of the many different branches of science. They are all well known for their work, but they have not been chosen because they are the "greatest" Canadian scientists. It would be very difficult to pick the six greatest, especially as more than ten Canadian scientists have won the **Nobel Prize**.

Thousands of Canadian scientists deserve to be called "great," including the people you will read about here. To learn about other great Canadian scientists, consult the reading list at the end of this book.

1891–1941

Frederick Banting and Charles Best *1899–1978*

> **❝** He [Best] has assisted me in all the operations and taught me the chemistry so that we work together all the time and check up on each other's readings. **❞**
>
> *Frederick Banting*

Key Events

1916 Fred graduates in medicine and joins the army
Charley breaks off his studies at the University of Toronto in order to join the army

1918 Fred is wounded at the battle of Cambrai, France

1919 Charley resumes his studies in physiology and biochemistry
Fred is a resident in surgery at the Hospital for Sick Children, Toronto

1920 Fred opens an office in London, Ontario

1921 Fred and Charley discover how to produce insulin

1922 Fred opens an office in Toronto to treat patients who have diabetes

1923 Fred and John Macleod are awarded the Nobel Prize for physiology and medicine

1929 Charley is appointed professor of physiology at the University of Toronto

1934 Fred is knighted

1939 Fred is appointed co-ordinating chairman of Canada's wartime medical research

Early Years

It was by accident that Fred Banting decided to become a doctor. During his early childhood, he had no great plans for his life. He was not even a good student. He preferred to be out in the shed, helping with the animals on his parents' farm near Alliston, Ontario.

The accident happened when Fred was walking home from school one day. He stopped to watch two men fix a roof—and suddenly the platform the men were standing on crashed to the ground. In a panic, Fred ran to get a doctor. Later, as he watched the doctor bind the men's wounds, Fred thought how wonderful it must be to have such skill and knowledge. Then and there, he decided to become a doctor.

Charley Best did not need an accident to convince him of the importance of medicine. He knew all about it because his father was a doctor. Charley grew up in Maine, in the United States, but he attended high school and university in Toronto. That was where he later met Fred Banting.

> " I watched every movement of those skillful hands as the doctor examined the injured men and tended to cuts, bruises and broken bones.... From that day it was my greatest ambition to be a doctor. "
> *Frederick Banting*

Fred was a fair student, but his teachers never thought he would become a famous scientist.

Backgrounder

Fred and Charley

Frederick Grant Banting and Charles Herbert Best both liked to be called by their nicknames—Fred and Charley. They had very different characters. Charley was a good-natured person who made friends easily. Fred was more reserved. He had a quick temper and was easily offended.

Developing Skills

Fred was halfway through his medical training in Toronto when World War I broke out in 1914. Like the rest of his class, Fred joined the army as soon as he graduated. He was sent overseas, and before long he was on a battlefield in France. There Fred tended wounded soldiers—until he was wounded in the arm.

Back in Canada after the war, Fred opened a doctor's office in London, Ontario. He was far from busy. As a new doctor in town, he had very few patients. To fill the time, he studied at home, reading about new developments in medicine. That was how he came to read an article about the pancreas.

The pancreas is a giant gland near the stomach that helps digest food. It also has another function. It contains clusters of cells called the "islets of Langerhans"—because they look like islands in a sea of tissue. These islets release the substance that we now call **insulin**. Many scientists had tried to find this substance, for they knew it was needed by people with diabetes. Yet there seemed to be no way of separating the substance from the rest of the pancreas.

During World War I, Fred was sent to Europe to work in an army hospital even though he had not yet finished medical school.

Backgrounder

Diabetes

Diabetes is the common name for *diabetes mellitus*. People who suffer from diabetes lack a substance called insulin.

When food is digested, some of it becomes glucose (a sugar) and is moved through the bloodstream to give energy to all the cells in the body. People whose bodies lack insulin cannot convert glucose into energy. The glucose remains in the blood. Unless they are given insulin, they get very thin and weak, and eventually die. Today, people with diabetes can live long and healthy lives with the aid of insulin. This was not the case when Fred and Charley started their experiments. There was no good treatment for diabetes. If you had diabetes, you died.

The article that caused Fred such excitement explained that if the tubes leading to the pancreas are tied off (causing the pancreas to shrivel and dry up), most of the islets of Langerhans remain intact. The islets continue to produce the special substance, or insulin. Fred thought this might be a way of obtaining the substance in a pure form.

He took his idea to Professor John J. R. Macleod, who was head of physiology at the University of Toronto. John was not encouraging. He told Fred that scientists had been working on this subject for years. Some had made an extract from the pancreas and injected it into patients. There had always been bad side effects: sickness, dizziness, pain, and sometimes death.

Fred still thought his idea might work, and eventually John let him have his way. He introduced Fred to Charley Best, a fourth-year student in physiology and biochemistry. The two could do experiments during the summer, said John. They could work in a room in the physiology department.

Charley and another student flipped a coin to see who would work with Frederick Banting through the summer holidays. Charley won, and he started working on a cure for diabetes.

Accomplishments

Fred and Charley began their experiments on May 17, 1921. To begin with, John was available to give them advice. But in mid-June, he went on his summer holidays, leaving Fred and Charley to carry on alone.

It was slow, painstaking work. At the beginning of each experiment, Fred removed the pancreas of a dog so that the dog developed diabetes. A week or so later, he and Charley injected the dog with an extract they had made from the pancreas of another dog. They soon found that they could make a good extract from the pancreas without tying it off and making it shrivel.

By the time John returned from his holidays, Fred and Charley were making dogs better by injecting them with insulin. But the whole thing was very hit and miss. Sometimes the insulin worked well. Sometimes it did not—it was too strong or too weak. Realizing how much still had to be done, John added more researchers to the team, including James Collip. It was James who found a way of **purifying** the insulin so that it was reliable enough to use on humans.

At the beginning of their study, seven out of ten dogs died during operations. Fred and Charley soon learned better methods to use **anesthetic**, and more dogs survived.

Backgrounder

Animals and Research

Many people think it is wrong to do experiments on animals. Unfortunately, some experiments have to be done on living creatures. Fred and Charley could not have discovered insulin without using animals. It is true that more than a dozen dogs died because of their research. It is also true that millions of people throughout the world have remained alive and active because of this research.

Already by 1922, the researchers had found that they did not have to use the pancreas of dogs to make insulin. Beef or pork pancreas, when ground up, made a very good base for the extract. Beef pancreas was particularly plentiful because of all the cattle killed for meat. Today, insulin is made from modified **yeast**.

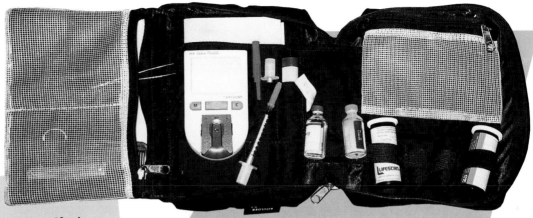

Today, insulin kits such as this are given to diabetics around the world.

> *I tested the effect of the extract on a depancreatized dog whose blood sugar was 460 mg percent. Following the injection, the percentage fell to almost normal and the condition of the dog improved in an astonishing manner.*
> Frederick Banting

The first person to receive insulin was a fourteen-year-old boy who was dying of diabetes. His treatment began in January 1922, and by May he was well enough to leave hospital. The year 1922 was a miraculous one for people with diabetes. With insulin injections twice a day, they could look forward to long and active lives.

The following year, Fred and John were awarded the Nobel Prize, one of the world's greatest honours. Instead of being pleased, Fred was furious. He said Charley deserved the prize more than John, and he gave half of his prize money to Charley. John shared his half with James Collip.

Fred went on to do further research on diabetes, but he was killed in a plane crash during World War II. Charley became a professor at the University of Toronto, where he made another important discovery. He developed a substance called heparin, which prevents blood from clotting. It is partly because of heparin that surgeons can now do long and complex operations.

▶▶▶▶▶▶

QUICK NOTES

▶ Fred was awarded the Military Cross for treating wounded soldiers at the battle of Cambrai (1918) when shells were exploding all around him.

▶ Charley also served in World War I. He was a sergeant in the artillery.

▶ Fred's honours included a knighthood. He became Sir Frederick Banting.

1945–

Roberta Bondar

> " As I look down, across, and above the flight-deck window, the shining planet curves from left to right. I have never in my life seen anything as big as this. "

Key Events

1968 Earns a bachelor of science degree in zoology and agriculture

1971 Earns a master's degree in experimental pathology

1974 Earns a Ph.D. in neurobiology

1977 Earns an M.D.

1982 Appointed assistant professor of medicine, McMaster University

1983 Is accepted into the Canadian space program

1988 Joins the staff of Sunnybrook Medical Centre, Toronto

1992 Becomes first Canadian woman and second Canadian astronaut to go into space

1993–96 Is chairperson for the Friends of the Environment Foundation

Early Years

"**G**irls! Your space helmets have arrived!" shouted Roberta's mother. Roberta and her sister Barbara rushed downstairs to open the parcels that had come. The helmets were rectangles of white cardboard. As Roberta pulled hers over her head, she could not help feeling disappointed. Although she was only eight years old, she knew that a real space helmet would not look like this.

Roberta had been interested in space as far back as she could remember. At her home in Sault Ste. Marie, Ontario, she made plastic models of rockets and satellites. She and Barbara built their own "space station" and pretended to be space travellers discovering strange planets.

As Roberta grew older, she stopped playing such games. But she never lost her fascination with space. Someday, somehow, she was determined to get there.

Roberta was always a top student. She won high school science competitions, and went on to earn five university degrees.

Backgrounder

An Early Experience

Roberta found out early in life that girls were not always treated the same as boys. In Grade 8, she came top in the test for school crossing guards, and she expected to be made safety patrol captain. But the boy who came second in the test was made captain. From then on, Roberta was determined to prove that she could do everything as well as any boy—if not better.

Developing Skills

Roberta was sixteen when Yuri Gagarin circled Earth in a spaceship. As more and more astronauts were sent into space, Roberta followed every detail. She was especially pleased when the Soviet Union sent up a woman astronaut—Valentina Tereshkova.

Roberta knew that anyone picked for a space mission would have to have a great many skills. She set out to learn these skills. First, she studied for a bachelor of science degree. Then she worked for three more degrees—in **pathology**, **neurobiology**, and medicine. Then she did further training. All this took many years. Roberta was thirty-six by the time she had completed her training. By then, she was also a pilot, having learned to fly a plane.

As a fully qualified doctor, Roberta was appointed an assistant professor of medicine at McMaster University in Hamilton, Ontario. She had not been there long when her big chance came. Listening to the radio one day, she heard that Canada was starting a program for astronauts. Anyone interested could apply. Roberta sent in her application the very next day.

Roberta was a strong athlete. She knew anyone going into space had to be physically fit.

More than 4,300 men and women applied to be trained as astronauts. Only six were chosen, and only one of them was a woman. The woman was Roberta. At last her dream was coming true! Yet she knew that this was only the beginning. The training program would be tougher than anything she had done so far.

Since Canadian astronauts would be flying in an American spacecraft, much of the training was in the United States. At the National Aeronautics and Space Administration (NASA), the six Canadians went on practice flights in NASA's training jet. This was to get their bodies used to the weightlessness of space. All six tried hard to prove their worth. They knew that only one of them would be chosen to go on the space shuttle in 1984. Who would the lucky person be? It was Marc Garneau, a naval commander who was a specialist in electrical engineering.

> 66 *I've spent five years of high school, eighteen years of university, eight years in the Canadian Astronaut Program, and three years of book work and practice preparing for this flight.* 99

Once Roberta became part of the Canadian Space Agency, she was sent to NASA to train as an astronaut.

Backgrounder

The Space Program

The first person to go into space was Yuri Gagarin, a Soviet astronaut. He circled the Earth twice in April 1961. Less than a month later, Alan Shepard became the first American in space, though he did not go into **orbit**. John Glenn was the first American to orbit the Earth (in 1962). The other early astronauts were all Americans or Soviets. The United States and Soviet Union were the only countries that had this type of space program. Canada has aided space exploration in different ways. For instance, the Canadarm is a Canadian invention. This electro-mechanical arm allows astronauts to handle satellites and other objects that are floating in space.

Accomplishments

Roberta had to wait eight more years before she went on a space mission. But at last the great day came. On January 22, 1992, Roberta and six other astronauts were blasted into space aboard the American space shuttle, *Discovery*.

Roberta tried to seem calm, but she was tremendously excited. As soon as the shuttle was in orbit, she unstrapped herself from her seat and floated toward a window. There she had her first sight of Earth. It seemed to glow with light. Its atmosphere was a shimmering blue. Then Roberta saw other colours as well—the red of deserts, the green of forests. The Earth was a ball of colour. Almost everything else in the universe was black—a deep, deep black.

> *The most thrilling moment was looking at Earth.... It comes at you out of the black universe.*

As Roberta gazed out the window, she barely had time to recognize one country before she was passing another. The shuttle was travelling at 8 kilometres (5 miles) per second. It took only ninety minutes to do a complete orbit of Earth. Roberta could happily have gazed at Earth for hours on end, but she was not just a passenger. She had work to do.

Roberta had to conduct her experiments while being weightless in space.

Backgrounder

A Patriotic Canadian

Roberta loves Canada and is proud to be Canadian. The first time the shuttle flew over the country, Roberta played a tape of "O Canada." Later, she stopped work to take a quick look out the window when the shuttle passed over Canada. "When you see your own country from space, it is an extraordinary experience," she says.

Roberta was named to the Canadian Medical Hall of Fame in 1998.

During the eight days of the flight, Roberta performed a number of experiments. She spent a lot of time working at the glove box. This is a tightly closed box especially designed for experiments in space. Astronauts can do experiments inside the box by putting their hands in a pair of gloves, but nothing can get out of the box. Chemicals and soil particles cannot escape and float around the shuttle.

Another of Roberta's jobs was to examine her fellow astronauts, especially their backbones. A person's backbone stretches when there is no force of gravity pulling at it. Roberta has continued this type of work since her return to Earth. She does research on the effect space has on astronauts. Some astronauts feel very dizzy after a space flight. Others have painful back aches.

Roberta has been involved in many projects during the last few years. A number of years ago, Roberta was described as a human whirlwind. Today, she is still a whirlwind of activity. One month, she is working in New Mexico. The next month she is giving lectures in Ottawa. One of Roberta's main concerns is the environment. From 1993 to 1996, she was chairperson of the Friends of the Environment Foundation. Roberta's space flight made her realize how important it is to protect Earth from harm.

▶▶▶▶▶▶

QUICK NOTES

▶ The Soviet Space Agency invited Roberta to go on a space flight in 1991. She turned down the offer because she would not be a working member of the crew. She would be a "human laboratory rat." The Russians wanted to study how long-term weightlessness affected a woman.

▶ Roberta took a lot of taped music to play on the space shuttle. The tapes included works by Canadian artists, a high school band, and Girl Guide songs.

▶ Roberta's web site is http://www.ns. sympatico.ca/Features /Road/bondar.html.

1946–

Biruté Galdikas

> 66 Orangutans were everywhere: ambling along the paths in camp, lounging on the steps of our house, napping in the rafters, hanging on my body, crowding my thoughts. 99

Key Events

1966 Earns a bachelor of arts degree

1969 Earns a master's degree in anthropology

1971 Arrives in Borneo and starts work at Camp Leakey

1978 Receives a doctor's degree in anthropology

1980 Is appointed a part-time professor at Simon Fraser University

1993 Receives United Nations Global 500 Award

1995 Publishes *Reflections of Eden: My Years with the Orangutans of Borneo*

1997 Is awarded the Tyler Prize by the University of Southern California

Early Years

Biruté was about six when she first went to a library and took out a book. The book was *Curious George*, the story of an explorer and his banana-eating monkey. Biruté thought she would like to be an explorer. Her family lived near High Park in Toronto, and she spent a lot of time "exploring" the park.

By the time Biruté was in high school, she had become fascinated by apes. She pored over books about them for hours on end. Her favourites were orangutans—the red apes of Asia.

When Biruté was nineteen, she heard about Jane Goodall, who was studying chimpanzees in Africa. Jane was actually living among chimpanzees in the forest. Biruté had not realized such a thing was possible. She now had a new ambition—to live among orangutans.

> " I dreamed of going to the great forests of the Far East to study orangutans. I was obsessed with the idea. "

Growing up in Toronto, Biruté (far right) was the oldest of four children.

Backgrounder

Biruté's Family

Biruté's parents, Antanas and Filomena Galdikas, were from Lithuania. Biruté was born in Germany when her parents were on their way to Canada. Biruté's younger sister and two brothers were all born in Canada.

Developing Skills

Biruté studied anthropology at the University of California at Los Angeles. She wanted to be well prepared to work with orangutans—if she ever managed to do so. That was the big problem. She could not just walk into the jungle with a notebook and camera. First, she had to get to Asia. She needed a sponsor who would help pay for the project.

Dian Fossey (left), Jane Goodall (middle), and Biruté are known as "Leakey women." Louis Leakey helped each of them set up their studies of primates.

During the next few years, Biruté was determined to find a way to study orangutans. She asked her professors for advice. She wrote to people in Asia. Nobody seemed able to help. Then, in 1969, Louis Leakey came to lecture at the university. Louis was the anthropologist who had arranged for Jane Goodall to study chimpanzees. He had also arranged for Dian Fossey to study mountain gorillas.

After the lecture, Biruté went up to Louis and said she wanted to study orangutans. They met again later, and eventually Louis decided to help her. But it would take time, he warned. It took almost three years. Biruté was twenty-five when she was finally able to go to Asia. By then she had married Rod Brindamour, a fellow Canadian.

Backgrounder

Anthropology

Anthropology is the study of human beings. Physical anthropologists are interested in the origin and evolution of human beings. Therefore, they are also interested in the great apes. By studying apes, they hope to learn about human behaviour and development.

> 66 *Human babies do not demand constant contact, nor do they cling in the same way.... At times it was nerve-wracking to have this little ball of orange fluff permanently attached to my body. But most of the time I was enchanted by my adopted infant.* 99

Biruté became a mother figure to orangutans rescued from captivity. Some even shared her meals, slept beside her, and travelled with her everywhere.

Louis had arranged for Biruté and Rod to do their work on the island of Borneo in Indonesia. They were to study the orangutans in Tanjung Puting reserve in the southwest part of the island. Very little was known about these orangutans—or, indeed, about any orangutans that were living in the wild.

Biruté and Rod travelled to the reserve by river in the pouring rain. The last part of the journey was in a dugout canoe. There were no roads in this thick rain forest. They were totally cut off from the world, with no electricity, telephone, or even mail. Their house was a thatched hut in a small clearing in the forest. Biruté was thrilled. This was just what she had hoped for. She named the place Camp Leakey.

Biruté was less happy once she had settled in. She could not find any orangutans. The apes lived high in the trees, hidden by the thick leaves. It was Christmas Eve when at last she spied a mother and baby. The baby looked like a small ball of orange fuzz, clinging to the spiky red-brown fur of its mother.

Accomplishments

As the months passed, Biruté saw many more orangutans. She gave each a name and kept a record of its activities. She usually heard the ape before she saw it. Sometimes she heard a male make a long call. More often, the sound of branches crashing told her that orangutans were moving around high above her.

When an orangutan came down low enough to be seen, Biruté followed it all day. She did not leave until it made a nest in the branches and settled down for the night. The next morning, Biruté went back to the nest and again followed the ape. She soon developed a sore neck from looking up all the time, and she was often soaking wet. The ground would be water-logged during the rainy season, and Biruté had to wade through waist-high swamps.

As well as studying wild orangutans, Biruté rescued some that had been kept as pets. Having a pet orangutan was against the law in Indonesia, but nobody took much notice. The pets were usually kept in cages and did not live long. They soon perked up when they came to Camp Leakey and could move around freely.

Orangutans were constant companions for Biruté as she worked in her jungle home.

❝ *I hope [I can] help people understand orangutans and their tropical rain forest world, a world which is in grave danger of vanishing forever.* **❞**

Before long, Biruté had quite a crowd of orangutans at Camp Leakey. At first, they tended to stay near the camp—or near Biruté. One baby orangutan clung to her shoulder day and night. It stayed with her when she followed wild orangutans through the forest. It would not even let go when she wanted to wash.

Having orangutans at the camp gave Biruté a chance to study them closely. But she also learned a lot about the wild orangutans. When she wrote her **doctoral thesis**, it was packed with information. As a result of the thesis, Biruté was appointed a part-time professor at Simon Fraser University in British Columbia. She continued to live at Camp Leakey, but she went to Canada each year to give lectures.

Biruté still spends most of her time at Camp Leakey. The camp has changed a lot since she first arrived. It now has many more buildings and people. Students go there to do fieldwork. Meanwhile, Biruté continues with her own work, especially with her efforts to save orangutans.

Biruté is considered the world's most knowledgeable person on orangutans.

Backgrounder

Saving Orangutans

In Tanjung Puting reserve, where Camp Leakey was established, the killing of orangutans was forbidden. But there was no law against cutting down trees. Each year, the forest area became smaller. Biruté has tried to prevent logging in the region. The orangutans cannot survive when their habitat is removed. They are safe in the trees but are easily caught on the ground.

Poachers and pet owners were also a threat to orangutans. Biruté has had an effect here as well. By taking the pets from their owners, she made sure they survived. More than 100 orangutans are now living in the forest because of her efforts. Camp Leakey was just a temporary home for them. They stayed there only until they were strong enough to fend for themselves in the forest.

1932–

Michael Smith

> **Most discoveries are made by people looking at something they are interested in and making an observation which may not have been directly what they were looking for.**

Key Events

1953 Earns a bachelor of science degree from the University of Manchester

1956 Earns a Ph.D. in chemistry from the University of Manchester

1956–60 Works for B.C. Research in Vancouver, British Columbia

1961 Becomes head of Vancouver Chemical Laboratory, Fisheries Research Board

1966 Joins Department of Biochemistry, University of British Columbia

1971 Is promoted to full professor, Department of Biochemistry

1975–76 Visits Laboratory of Molecular Biology, Medical Research Council, in England

1978 Publishes an account of his findings in the *Journal of Biological Chemistry*

1993 Is awarded the Nobel Prize in chemistry

1995 Is made a Companion of the Order of Canada

1997 Is made an honorary fellow of the Royal College of Physicians, England

Early Years

Michael was born in Blackpool, England. His father was a market gardener, and his mother had various jobs. Both parents worked hard to bring in enough money to feed and clothe Michael and his brother Robin.

When Michael was eleven, he won a scholarship to a private school. This was great news. It meant he would get a very good education—the type of education that prepares students for university. Michael's parents were delighted, but Michael was not. He was afraid he would feel out of place among children from wealthy homes.

Michael was not happy at the private school. He missed his friends, and he did not like having so much homework. He was not used to spending his evenings studying. In the end, it was worth the effort. At the age of eighteen, Michael won a scholarship to the University of Manchester.

Backgrounder

Biochemistry

Biochemistry is connected with both biology and chemistry. Biochemists study what goes on inside the cells of living things. Each cell is like a tiny chemical workshop. Biochemists study the **chromosomes**, **genes**, **DNA**, **proteins**, and other things that are at work inside each cell.

Developing Skills

Michael did well at Manchester, and in 1956 he received a Ph.D. in chemistry. He was hoping to do more research in chemistry and then get a job with a chemical company. But he could not get the type of research position he wanted. Then he heard that a biochemist in Vancouver was looking for a researcher. The biochemist was Har Gobind Khorana, who later won a Nobel Prize. At the time, he was doing research on certain important molecules. This was a more difficult type of chemistry than Michael was used to, but the work sounded interesting. As well, he liked the idea of living in Vancouver. So he packed his bags and **immigrated** to Canada.

Through his research, Michael became an expert on the DNA molecule. The DNA molecule is like a code that carries a set of instructions. Twisted strands of DNA form the genes that decide what any living thing will be like. They decide which characteristics will be passed from one generation to the next.

DNA determines all the characteristics a person will have.

> *One of the areas where genetic engineering is going to make an enormous impact is understanding how genes work.... I think that kind of understanding will lead to development of new anti-cancer drugs.*

The strands of DNA are so tiny that you need a very powerful microscope to see them. They look similar to a spiral staircase or a twisted ladder. Michael's work was connected with the "rungs" of the ladder. He was particularly interested in the fact that parts of the rungs sometimes changed position. When this happened, it caused an unusual change in the next generation.

Michael became such an expert on DNA that he was appointed professor at the University of British Columbia. A few years later, he took a leave of absence so that he could do some work at a laboratory in Cambridge, England. This laboratory was famous for its DNA research.

During a coffee break one day, when the Cambridge researchers were chatting, one of them said something that gave Michael an idea. They had been talking about the way bits of DNA could change position unexpectedly. Michael suddenly had the idea of actually making this happen. If scientists could find a way of changing DNA, all sorts of things might become possible. It could be a major step toward finding cures for cancer and other diseases.

Although Michael grew up in England, he now calls Canada home.

Backgrounder

Serendipity

Some of the greatest scientific discoveries have been made by accident. Scientists call this "serendipity." In Michael's case, the serendipity was triggered by his friend's remark during a coffee break. If his friend had not made that comment, Michael might never have thought of doing the research that led to his Nobel Prize.

Robert Noble is another Canadian scientist who made an important discovery because of something that happened by chance. But chance itself is not enough. It can only lead to a discovery if the scientist has the necessary background knowledge to realize what is happening. Without such knowledge, the opportunity will be missed.

Accomplishments

When Michael returned to Canada, he organized a team of researchers to work on his idea. He and his researchers found a way of changing DNA by doing experiments with chemicals in a test tube. They then took small bits of DNA out of a gene, changed the bits chemically, and put them back into the gene. Sometimes this seemed to have no result. Other times, their experiments caused a notable change.

By 1978, the experiments had gone so well that Michael wrote an article about his work. The article caused great excitement. Scientists all over the world began to use Michael's methods. "It's a whole new way of doing things," said one. "It will allow scientists to solve a lot of mysteries." It also gave scientists a new way of **breeding** crops and making medications.

> *This award [the Nobel Prize] shows that science done in British Columbia is as good as science done anywhere in the world.*

Michael's discoveries made it possible for scientists to change individual genes and to record the effect.

Backgrounder

Genetic Engineering

The type of changes Michael made in genes is called "genetic engineering." His first attempts were very much a matter of trial and error. Michael compared them to trying to fix the engine of a car without knowing much about cars. The car will not start, so you take off the blue door and replace it with a green door. The car still will not start. You then try replacing the tailpipe. Still the car will not start. Finally, you tighten the electric wire that leads to the spark plugs. The car starts.

In 1981, Michael formed a company so that his methods could be used to design new medications. The company found a better way of producing insulin. This improved insulin was soon widely available. Meanwhile, Michael went to work each day as usual. It was a big surprise, in 1993, when he heard on the radio that he had won the Nobel Prize in chemistry. He and an American scientist had been awarded the prize jointly.

Michael's share of the prize was $500,000. He gave it all away. Half went toward research on schizophrenia, a mental disorder. The rest went to help people learn more about science— especially to help women become scientists. This was typical of Michael's generosity. Michael owns a ski cabin in the mountains, and he has opened it to all the workers in his laboratory. All they have to do is say which weeks they want to go there.

When the news of Michael's Nobel Prize first became known, a lot of people said, "It couldn't have happened to a nicer guy." This is one of the secrets of Michael's success. His laboratory is a happy place, where people work together as a team. Even after winning the world's top prize in science, Michael refuses to behave like a star. He still works as hard as ever, eager to see what further results his research may bring.

Michael gave all of the Nobel Prize money that he won to researchers and science societies.

▶▶▶▶▶▶▶
QUICK NOTES

▶ Michael loves outdoor activities such as camping, hiking, skiing, and sailing.
▶ His love for camping began when he was a Boy Scout in England.
▶ Michael has three children, Tom, Ian, and Wendy.

1929–
Denis St-Onge

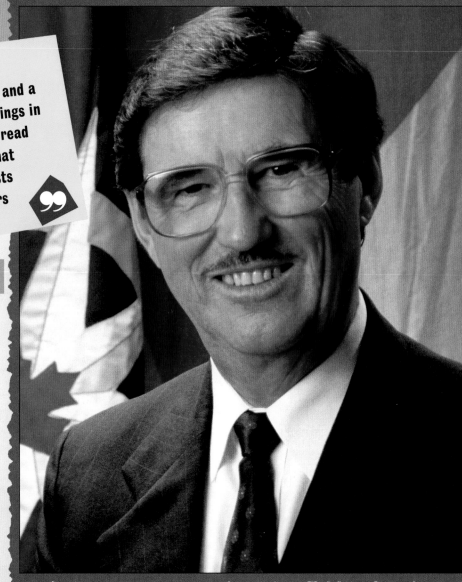

> 66 **The only difference between a geomorphologist and a historian is that we read things in a different way. Historians read manuscripts to find out what happened. Geomorphologists read sediments—the layers of clay, silt, and so on.** 99

Key Events

1953 Goes to Ethiopia

1957 Earns a master of science degree at the University of Louvain, Belgium

1959–61 Does research on Ellef Ringnes Island

1962 Earns a doctor of science degree

1965 Joins the Geological Survey of Canada as a research scientist

1968 Is appointed professor at University of Ottawa

1979–80 Is president of the Canadian Association of Geographers

1982 Returns to the Geological Survey of Canada

1984–85 Is president of the Geological Association of Canada

1992–98 Is president of the Royal Canadian Geographical Society

1996–97 Is president of the Canadian Geoscience Council

1997 Launches *Géographica*, the French edition of *Canadian Geographic* magazine

Early Years

"**H**ow come there are rocks in the river?" Denis asked his grandfather. He could not understand it. There was no rock anywhere else in the neighbourhood. Yet the river had huge boulders in it.

Denis lived on the banks of the Red River in the village of Ste-Agathe, Manitoba. His grandfather ran the ferry that took people across the river each summer. Denis was about six when he first began to help his grandfather on the ferry.

Denis loved working on the ferry. There was so much to see on the river. In spring, he watched grains of sand being moved along by melting ice. At other times, the waters flooded over the banks. Denis could see that rivers cause change, and he was always full of questions. How far had the river come? Where was it going? Although Denis did not realize it, he was learning **geography**.

Denis asked questions about the land and geography, even as a young boy.

Backgrounder

A Bilingual Upbringing

When Denis was a boy, all public schools in Manitoba had to teach in English. However, Denis's village of Ste-Agathe was a French-speaking community. There was only one English-speaking family in the whole village. As a result, the students were taught in French. Even so, most of them could speak English. English was all around them in Manitoba, especially on the radio. Denis loved to listen to *Hockey Night in Canada*.

Developing Skills

When Denis was thirteen, his parents sent him to the Juniorat. This was a Roman Catholic boarding school that prepared boys for university. Denis's father, who was a mechanic, could barely afford the fees, but he wanted Denis to have the chance to go to university.

In 1951, Denis earned a bachelor of arts degree from St-Boniface College, University of Manitoba. He then took a job as a teacher in Addis Ababa, the capital of Ethiopia. Addis was the other side of the world from Manitoba. That was partly why Denis chose to go there. He thought it would be an exciting adventure. It turned out to be more than an adventure. It changed Denis's life.

Denis learned about geography at the same time he taught it in Africa.

Denis had to teach geography to the students in Ethiopia. Although he had always been curious about geography, he had never studied it. Now he had to learn all the details. He was totally fascinated. So many of the things he had wondered about at last made sense. Denis knew he had found his true calling.

Ethiopia also changed Denis's life in another way. He met a Belgian dentist, Jeanne Behaegel, and within six months they were married. Jeanne's work as a dentist at the Imperial Hospital in Ethiopia paid for Denis's later studies in Belgium.

After returning to Canada, Denis worked on a French translation of the *Atlas of Canada*. While doing so, he heard that a program was being set up to send researchers to the Arctic. In 1959, Denis was chosen as one of the first six researchers to take part in the program. He was to study the geomorphology of Ellef Ringnes Island. This island was so far north that very few people had ever been there.

Denis conducted much of his fieldwork in the Northwest Territories.

Denis spent the next three summers on Ellef Ringnes Island. When he first arrived, he could not believe his eyes. It was not just that there was daylight all the time. Denis had expected that. But he had not expected to see nature in action—actually shaping the landscape. When the snow began to melt, the rivers roared and mud slides poured. Everything seemed to be moving. Denis was on the move too, racing around to record as many details as possible.

Backgrounder

Geomorphology

Geomorphology is the history of landscape—how the land has come to be the way it is today. When geomorphologists study an area, they "read" its history by studying the layers of clay, silt, gravel, and other materials in the soil. Each layer tells them what was happening at a particular time. By knowing the landscape so thoroughly, **geomorphologists** can tell how human activities, such as logging and mining, may affect an area.

Accomplishments

In 1962, Denis earned a doctor of science degree by writing a thesis about Ellef Ringnes Island. The thesis was an important piece of work. It gave new and surprising evidence about the way the Arctic landscape was formed. Denis had also invented a new type of mapping system to help geomorphologists show their findings clearly.

During the next few years Denis worked for the Geological Survey of Canada. He carried out geomorphological surveys in the dry desert of southwestern Saskatchewan and in the Swan Hills of Alberta. A lot of logging had been done in the Swan Hills, leaving the hills bare so that rain washed the soil away. The soil ended up in the rivers, which then affected the fish. The whole **ecosystem** of the region was affected by this logging. One of Denis's tasks was to find how this chain of events could be reduced when trees had to be cut down to leave space for road building.

> *You cannot fully appreciate the tundra unless you are entirely alone. Then you have total contact with nature. You hear the sounds of the wind, the birds, the animals. The only human sound is the sound of your feet.*

▶▶▶▶▶▶

Quick Notes

▶ Denis was the oldest child in a family of nine—six boys and three girls.

▶ Denis and his wife Jeanne have two children. Marc is a **geologist**, and Nicole is a historian.

▶ Denis's many honours include the Order of Canada, the Medal of the Royal Scottish Geographical Society, and the Medal of the University of Liège, Belgium.

Denis developed a unique method of mapping the surface of the Earth.

Denis shares his passion for science with his son Marc. They worked together in the Coppermine River Valley.

As a leading expert in his field, Denis was appointed a professor at the University of Ottawa in 1968. He later served as head of the Department of Geography and as vice-dean of the School of Graduate Studies. During these years, his son Marc trained to be a geologist. In 1981, Denis joined Marc on a survey he was doing in the Coppermine River Valley in the Northwest Territories. Once Denis was back studying the Arctic, he wondered why he had ever left it.

In 1982, Denis rejoined the Geological Survey of Canada to continue his Arctic studies. On his trip with Marc, he had discovered that when the ice was retreating in the Coppermine Valley, it had formed a huge lake. Nobody else had known about this glacial lake. During the next few years, Denis mapped all of the Coppermine Valley and made other surveys in the region. In 1988, Denis took a group of international geologists on a raft trip down the Coppermine River to show them the glacial lake and some of his other findings.

Denis was president of the Royal Canadian Geographical Society from 1992 to 1998. He has been involved in many other organizations. He still spends a great deal of time helping Canadians learn more about their country. Denis believes that one way of getting to know Canada is by going on field trips. "Physical geography," he says, "is something you learn through your feet, not through your head."

Backgrounder

The Beauty of the Tundra

The Coppermine River Valley is in the Arctic region known as the tundra. The tundra is not a desert like the islands of the High Arctic. It is a colourful region, where flowers grow in summer. There are hundreds of lakes, and little streams that bubble and sing as they flow along. Musk-oxen, caribou, bears, and wolves can be seen there, as well as many kinds of birds. "Walking in the tundra is absolutely magnificent," says Denis. He shares his love of the region by giving illustrated talks to schools and other groups.

1936–

David Suzuki

> **I've always regarded myself as merely a messenger of important information.**

Key Events

1942 David and his family are sent to an internment camp

1961 Earns a Ph.D. from the University of Chicago

1963 Joins the University of British Columbia (UBC)

1969 Is appointed professor of zoology at UBC

1971–72 Hosts *Suzuki on Science*

1974–79 Hosts *Science Magazine* (television) and *Quirks and Quarks* (radio)

1979 Launches *The Nature of Things with David Suzuki*

1985 Hosts the television show *A Planet for the Taking*

1986 Is awarded the UNESCO Kalinga prize for science

1987 Publishes life story, *Metamorphosis*

1992 Receives a Gemini Award as best host of a children's television series

1998 Publishes *Earth Time: Essays* and *The Amazing Seeds*

Early Years

When David was six, he and his family were forced to leave their home in Marpole, British Columbia. They had done nothing to deserve such treatment, but they were of Japanese origin, and Canada was at war with Japan.

David was too young to realize what was happening, but he did know he was Canadian. David's grandparents had come from Japan in the early 1900s. His parents were born in Canada, and so were David and his sisters. Although his family did follow some Japanese traditions, David did not even speak Japanese.

David's family was sent to a camp in the mountains, along with hundreds of other families. Some of the people in the camp felt very bitter, and their children spoke poorly of Canada. David always defended Canada. Even as a boy, David had the courage to stand up for what he considered important.

David competed in and won three public speaking contests. He finished third in another.

Backgrounder

Japanese Canadians in World War II

After Japan entered World War II in December 1941, all Japanese Canadians living on the coast of British Columbia were ordered to move inland. The government feared that if Japan invaded Canada, Japanese Canadians might help the invaders. There were no grounds for these fears. They were based on racism, not on proof. Nevertheless, more than 20,000 men, women, and children were taken from their homes and sent inland to camps in remote areas. They lost almost everything they had, because the government sold their fishing boats, farms, and businesses, as well as their homes. Many of the people treated in this way were Canadian citizens. Canada was their home. They had never lived anywhere else.

Developing Skills

When the war ended in 1945, David's family moved to a village near Windsor, Ontario. David had been an eager student at the camp in British Columbia, and he continued to take his schoolwork seriously. When he was fourteen, the family settled in London, Ontario, where David attended high school. He did so well that he won a scholarship to Amherst College in Massachusetts.

> The best part of science has always been in the search. The fun is in experimenting, designing new tricks, and often getting totally unexpected results that then lead in entirely new directions.

At Amherst, David's main subject was biology. He had become interested in biology years earlier, when his father first took him on fishing and camping trips. David learned a lot about nature on these trips. He had gathered a big collection of insects, which he carefully identified and labelled. David continued to study biology after graduating from Amherst in 1958. He worked for a further degree at the University of Chicago and then became a researcher at Oak Ridge, Tennessee.

David liked the excitement of scientific work in the United States. He met many people who were as absorbed in their work as he was in his. But there were things about the United States that David did not like. He did not like the racism—the unfair treatment of African Americans. As usual, he did not keep his opinions to himself. He spoke out boldly, and he joined the **civil rights** movement, which was trying to make life better for African Americans.

David's projects have taken him around the world, including Africa.

Finally, David decided he could not live in the United States. There was too much violence and hatred. He longed to be back home in Canada. In 1962, he took a position at the University of Alberta, and the following year he moved to the University of British Columbia. There he continued to both teach and research.

David's research was in genetics. This is the branch of biology that studies how characteristics are passed from one generation to the next. David studied generations of fruit flies—the tiny insects that hover around ripe fruit. Often, he was so excited by his research that he worked for fifteen hours at a stretch. Sometimes he stayed all night in his laboratory to finish an experiment. His hard work paid off. By the late 1960s, David had made some important discoveries. He was known throughout North America as a leading geneticist.

Backgrounder

David's Research on Fruit Flies

The common fruit fly is a good insect for geneticists to study because each fly has a large number of offspring, and they reproduce quickly. A fruit fly reproduces in less than two weeks. This means that many generations can be studied in a single year.

David managed to breed a strain of fruit fly that died in hot weather. This opened the door to all sorts of possibilities. For instance, if other insects could be made to die when the temperature rose, farmers might not have to spray chemicals on crops. David's work earned him a great reputation. Each year between 1969 and 1972, he was awarded the E. W. R. Steacie Memorial Fellowship as Canada's best research scientist under the age of thirty-five.

Accomplishments

David became so well known that he was invited to visit other countries as a researcher and lecturer. Although he enjoyed these visits, he soon stopped doing research. He was worried that his discoveries might be used in a harmful way. "Science does good things," he said. "But it also produced the **atomic bomb**."

Giving up research did not mean giving up teaching. David remained a professor at the University of British Columbia. He also began to teach a wider audience—the general public. Most people know very little about science, and this worried David. He thought: If people do not understand what scientists are doing, how can they be sure that the scientists' work will not cause harm?

Ever since 1962, David had appeared occasionally on television and radio. In the early 1970s, he became very involved in broadcasting. He saw it as the perfect medium for explaining science to a large number of non-scientists. He began with the television series *Suzuki on Science*. It was followed by *Science Magazine*, a lively program that looked at everything from moon rocks to wheelchairs that climb stairs.

> *When I realized what a powerful medium television was, I saw it as a means of educating people about the importance and implications of science.*

David's accomplishments are recognized worldwide. He was awarded an honorary doctorate from Griffiths University in Brisbane, Australia.

Backgrounder

The David Suzuki Foundation

This organization is a non-profit group. Its members are people who care about the environment. The aim of the foundation is "to design a vision of Earth in which humans live within the planet's productive capacity." To find out more about this project and how you can help care for the environment, send an Email to solutions@davidsuzuki.org.

David's greatest commitment is to his family. He wants to teach his children to learn about and to love nature and science.

▶▶▶▶▶▶
QUICK NOTES

▶ David is a twin. He was born a few minutes before his sister Marcia. He has two other sisters, Aiko and Dawn.

▶ The village of Marpole, where David was born, is now part of Vancouver.

▶ David and his sisters are *Sansei* (third-generation Canadians). Their parents are *Nisei* (second-generation Canadians). Their grandparents, the people who came to Canada from Japan, are *Issei* (first-generation Canadians).

▶ David has five children—three from his first marriage and two from his second.

At the same time, David launched the popular radio show, *Quirks and Quarks.* Over the years, David has hosted a wide range of science programs. His best-known television series is *The Nature of Things with David Suzuki.* For twenty years, David has been the host of this show, which is immensely popular in other countries as well as in Canada.

The Nature of Things often looks at the way humans affect the environment. David is very concerned about the harm being done to our planet. He tries to educate people so that they cause as little harm as possible while going about their daily lives. Many of David's newspaper articles deal with this subject. David has written hundreds of newspaper articles, as well as a number of books. His book for children called *The Amazing Seeds* includes a packet of seeds so readers can grow their own trees.

David's work has brought him many awards and honours. It has also brought him criticism. His views about the environment are not always popular. Factory owners, for instance, do not like being told that they are polluting the rivers. This does not stop David. He continues to speak out for important issues, just as he did when he was a child.

MORE GREAT CANADIANS

Here are some more Canadian scientists. These accounts of their work will give you an idea of some of the ways scientists can use their knowledge. The scientists described here are only a few of the many. The Suggested Reading list will help you find more.

1909–1983

Henri Breault

Pediatrician

Henri has saved thousands of children from being poisoned each year. He was head of the Poison Control Centre at the Hotel-Dieu hospital in Windsor, Ontario. Every day, young children were brought to him for treatment. Some had drunk their parents' medicine. Others had swallowed cleaning fluid they had found in a kitchen cupboard. Henri arranged for a company to design a child-proof container with a cap that was hard to open. As soon as it came into use, the number of poisonings dropped by 91 percent. Child-proof containers are now used throughout the world.

1918–

Bertram Brockhouse

Nuclear Physicist

In 1994, Bert was awarded the Nobel Prize in physics for developing the triple-axis **neutron** spectrometer. This instrument allows scientists to see what is inside metals, minerals, gems, and rocks. It uses a neutron beam as a kind of flashlight to see inside these structures. Bert, who was born in Alberta, did his research at Chalk River, Ontario, while working for the Atomic Energy Project.

1907–

Donald Coxeter

Mathematician

Donald was professor of mathematics at the University of Toronto. He has been called "the world's greatest living classical **geometer**." Donald developed new theories of geometry, which he described in a number of books. Two of his most famous books are *Non-Euclidean Geometry* and *Regular Complex Polytopes*.

Bertram Brockhouse

1921–

Ursula Franklin

*Physicist and
Environmentalist*

Ursula was the first woman to be a professor at the University of Toronto. She is an expert on the structure of metals. By analyzing ancient tools and other objects, she can say when they were made. Ursula has also done research on the effects of nuclear fallout. She is very worried about the dangers of nuclear testing, and she has gained a worldwide reputation as a promoter of Science for Peace.

1919–

Jacques Genest

*Physician and Clinical
Researcher*

Born and raised in Montreal, Jacques is known especially for his ground-breaking research on high blood pressure. This condition is a major cause of heart attacks and strokes, which kill many people every year. Much of this research was done at the Clinical Research Institute, which Jacques founded and directed in Montreal.

Gerhard Herzberg

1904–1999

Gerhard Herzberg

Physicist

Gerhard is known as the father of molecular spectroscopy—the study of patterns of light given off by atoms and molecules. Born in Germany, he spent most of his working life at the National Research Council in Ottawa. In 1971, Gerhard was awarded the Nobel Prize in chemistry for his work on the structure of molecules.

1946–

Tak Mak

Immunobiologist

Tak was born in China and raised in Hong Kong. He immigrated to Canada in the late 1960s. Working at the Ontario Cancer Institute, Tak studied the body's immune system—the way the body fights disease. In 1984, he discovered how the cells in the body's immune system recognize invading cells and why these defences go wrong in the case of cancer. This important discovery led to new treatments for leukemia and other illnesses of the immune system.

1910–

Robert Noble

Physiologist

When Robert was director of the Collip Medical Research Laboratory at the University of Western Ontario, he made an important discovery by accident. His brother Clark, who was a doctor, sent him some leaves of the Madagascar periwinkle plant. Clark had received the leaves from a patient in Jamaica, who said that periwinkle tea was used as a treatment for diabetes when no insulin was available.

Robert tried out the leaves and found they had no effect on diabetes. But they did have a dramatic effect on controlling the growth of white blood cells. With great excitement, Robert set to work with fellow researchers to make an extract from the leaves. It took them several years, but eventually they produced a purified extract that was highly effective in treating certain types of cancer.

1929–

John Polanyi

Chemist

Born in Germany and educated in England, John has been a professor at the University of Toronto since the 1950s. In 1986, he won the Nobel Prize in chemistry for his research on how the behaviour of molecules brings about chemical change. His discoveries made it possible to build a new type of laser—a chemical laser.

As well as keeping up a busy research schedule, John is an active member of the Canadian Center for Arms Control and Disarmament. He has written many articles about the dangers of nuclear war. John believes it is important for scientists to take part in public affairs, especially those connected with science.

1905–1993

Helen Sawyer Hogg

Astronomer

Helen was a world-famous authority on globular clusters—groups of stars that are close together. A minor planet was named Sawyer Hogg in her honour. In addition to her scientific work, Helen wrote the popular book *The Stars Belong to Everyone*, and she gave talks on radio and television.

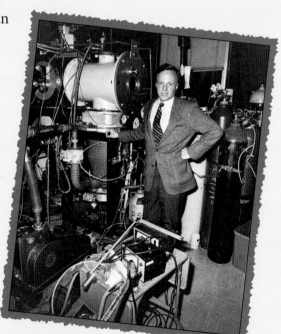

John Polanyi

Bonnie Schmidt

Science Promoter and Physiologist

In 1997, the *Financial Post* named Bonnie one of Canada's "Top 40 under 40." Bonnie is the founder and national director of Let's Talk Science. She formed the organization because she believes that Canadians do not know enough about science. Her aim is to help many more Canadians become "scientifically literate." Bonnie and her group are especially interested in encouraging young people to take up science. They design programs and give talks to elementary schools to show that science can be fascinating—and a lot of fun. Their web site is http://www.uwo.ca/letstalkscience.

Amanda Vincent

Lap-Chee Tsui

Molecular Geneticist

Molecular geneticists try to understand the structure and function of genes. Lap-Chee studied biology at the Chinese University of Hong Kong and began to specialize in genetics after he moved to North America. In 1983, Lap-Chee went to Toronto, where he did research on genes at the Hospital for Sick Children. There he discovered the gene that causes cystic fibrosis. Cystic fibrosis is a life-threatening disease that children inherit. Now that scientists know which gene causes the disease, they may be able to find better treatment for it. In the meantime, they can do tests to find out if parents are likely to produce a child with cystic fibrosis.

Amanda Vincent

Marine Biologist

Amanda is a professor at McGill University and the world's leading expert on the seahorse. This fascinating little creature is dying out, and Amanda is trying to save it. She and other conservationists have formed Project Seahorse, an international organization that is trying to prevent large numbers of seahorses from being killed by fishermen and passing ships. As part of this effort, Amanda and the local villagers have netted off a stretch of sea in the Philippines to make a "park" where seahorses can live safely. The film *The Secret Life of Seahorses* was made about this project. The web site of Project Seahorse is http://www.seahorse.mcgill.ca/.

GLOSSARY

anesthetic: a substance that puts a person or animal to sleep for the purpose of surgery

apothecary: someone who makes medications

atomic bomb: a bomb that uses the energy released when atoms are split rapidly

botanist: a scientist who studies plants

breeding: the producing of offspring

chromosome: a thread-like structure at the centre of each cell in a living thing

civil rights: the rights of a member of a country

DNA: an acid that is part of all living things

doctoral thesis: a long essay based on original research presented to earn a doctorate degree

ecosystem: a system where all living things interact in a certain environment

engineer: a person trained in any branch of engineering

gene: part of a cell that carries the characteristics of the living organism

geography: the science that studies the Earth's surface, or its peoples and resources

geologist: a scientist who studies the Earth's crust and its history

geometer: a person whose work is the study of geometry

geomorphologist: a scientist who studies Earth's surface

immigrate: to go and live in a country where one was not born

insulin: a substance secreted in the body enabling the body to use sugar

neurobiology: the study of the brain

neutron: a microscopic particle found in the nucleus of an atom

Nobel Prize: an honourable prize given in the fields of physics, chemistry, physiology and medicine, literature, economic sciences, and the promotion of peace

orbit: the curved path of a planet, satellite, or object around another in space

pathology: the study of the nature, causes, and effects of disease

protein: a complex compound that is a necessary part of the cells of animals and plants

purify: to make something pure, not mixed with anything else

yeast: a substance consisting mostly of cells of very small fungi

SUGGESTED READING

Bondar, Barbara. *On the Shuttle: Eight Days in Space.* Toronto: Greey de Pencier, 1993.

Black, Harry S. *Canadian Scientists and Inventors: Biographies of People Who Made a Difference.* Markham: Pembroke, 1997.

Gallardo, Evelyn. *Among the Orangutans: The Biruté Galdikas Story.* San Francisco: Chronicle Books, 1993.

Mrozewski, Jo. *Frederick Banting: Discovery of Insulin.* Mississauga: Copp Clark Pitman, 1991.

Shell, Barry. *Great Canadian Scientists.* Victoria: Polestar, 1997.

Webb, Michael. *Helen Sawyer Hogg: A Lifetime of Stargazing.* Mississauga: Copp Clark Pitman, 1991.

Webb, Michael. *Roberta Bondar: Leading Science into Space.* Mississauga: Copp Clark Pitman, 1993.

INDEX